EDGE BOOKS

⟶ THE GREAT OUTDOORS ⟵

DUCK HUNTING

Revised and Updated

by Randy Frahm

Consultant:
Paul Beinke
Chapter President
Minnesota Waterfowl Association
Owner, http://www.redbearhunting.com
Mankato, Minnesota

Capstone
press

Mankato, Minnesota

Edge Books are published by Capstone Press,
151 Good Counsel Drive, P.O. Box 669, Mankato, Minnesota 56002.
www.capstonepress.com

Library of Congress Cataloging-in-Publication Data
Frahm, Randy.
    Duck hunting / by Randy Frahm.—Rev. and updated.
    p. cm.—(Edge Books. The great outdoors)
    Includes bibliographical references and index.
    ISBN-13: 978-1-4296-0818-3 (hardcover)
    ISBN-10: 1-4296-0818-8 (hardcover)
1. Duck shooting—Juvenile literature. I. Title. II. Series.
SK333.D8F73 2008
799.2'44—dc22   2007011525

Summary: Describes the equipment, skills, conservation issues, and safety concerns of
duck hunting.

Editorial Credits
Carrie A. Braulick, editor; Katy Kudela, photo researcher; Tom Adamson, revised
    edition editor; Thomas Emery, revised edition designer; Kyle Grenz, revised
    edition production designer

Photo Credits
Capstone Press/Gary Sundermeyer, 5, 11, 14, 23, 26, 35; Gregg Andersen, 12, 21;
    Karon Dubke, 8
Gene Boaz, 17
Mark Raycroft, 29 (all)
Photri-Microstock/Leonard Lee Rue III, 32; Louie Bunde, 37
Rob and Ann Simpson, 7
Root Resources/Jim Flynn, 42
Shutterstock/C. Paquin, cover; Kirk Geisler, 44
Tom Stack & Associates/Barbara Gerlach, 41
Unicorn Stock Photos/Chris Brown, 31
Visuals Unlimited/Hank Andrews, 24; Cheryl A. Ertelt, 40; Gary C. Will, 43
William H. Mullins, 19

1 2 3 4 5 6 12 11 10 09 08 07

TABLE OF CONTENTS

Essential content terms are highlighted and are defined at the bottom of the page where they first appear.

Chapter 1

DUCK HUNTING

Learn about the history of duck hunting, types of ducks, and duck migration.

Duck hunting is one of the most popular forms of hunting. Ducks are common throughout North America. They live on marshes, rivers, lakes, and oceans.

Most people hunt ducks for food and recreation. They duck hunt to enjoy the outdoors or to spend time with friends and family. Many duck hunters enjoy the challenge of shooting at moving targets.

History of Duck Hunting

During the 1600s and 1700s, American Indians and early North American settlers hunted ducks. They ate the birds' meat and decorated their clothing with duck feathers. Market hunters sold duck meat and feathers for profit. These hunters shot ducks year-round. They killed as many ducks as they could.

Many duck hunters hunt for food and recreation.

By the late 1800s, people realized market hunters were killing too many ducks. By 1900, market hunting became illegal in North America.

Today, few duck hunters hunt for profit. Duck hunters hunt for recreation. They follow rules to maintain healthy duck populations.

Puddle Ducks

Two main types of ducks live throughout North America. These types are puddle ducks and diving ducks.

Puddle ducks are the most commonly hunted North American ducks. North American puddle duck species include mallards, wood ducks, and blue- and green-winged teals. Their habitats are small bodies of water, such as ponds and marshes.

Puddle ducks eat aquatic plants. These plants grow in the water. They also eat field crops, such as wheat and soybeans. Puddle ducks' legs are located near the center of their bodies. This placement helps the ducks walk on land to eat field crops.

species—a group of animals with similar features

Wood ducks are a type of puddle duck.

Diving Ducks

North American duck hunters hunt diving duck species, such as canvasbacks, redheads, goldeneyes, and ringneck ducks. Diving ducks have habitats on large bodies of water, such as rivers, lakes, and oceans. Many diving ducks live on the Atlantic and Pacific Oceans.

Orange Duck

Ingredients:
4 duck breasts
1 quart (1 liter) orange juice
1 cup (240 mL) diced onions
1 cup (240 mL) diced carrots
2 crushed garlic cloves
1 teaspoon (5 mL) pepper
¼ teaspoon (1.2 mL) nutmeg
¼ teaspoon (1.2 mL) thyme leaves

Equipment:
Slow cooker

1. Place duck breasts in slow cooker.

2. Add all other ingredients to slow cooker.

3. Place cover on slow cooker and simmer for 6 hours at 250 degrees Fahrenheit (120 degrees Celsius) or until duck breasts are tender.

Diving ducks dive and swim to find food. They mainly eat small fish. Some of these ducks also eat aquatic plants.

Migration

Most ducks migrate each year during the fall. Ducks move to escape the cold winter weather and to find food. Many ducks hatched in Canada fly to Mexico. Mexico has a much warmer climate than Canada and most of the United States. Each spring, the ducks fly from Mexico back to Canada to nest. These ducks then lay eggs and raise their young. Ducks usually follow natural features such as seacoasts or rivers as they migrate.

Ducks are strong, fast flyers. They fly between 35 and 50 miles (56 and 80 kilometers) per hour as they migrate. Migrating ducks can travel 1,000 to 1,500 miles (1,600 to 2,400 kilometers) in a few days.

migrate—to fly away to live in a different region

Chapter 2

EQUIPMENT

Learn about shotguns, shells, decoys, blinds, and more.

Duck hunters need a lot of equipment with them on their hunt. Besides something to shoot the ducks, they need equipment that will attract ducks and prevent ducks from seeing them.

Shotguns

Hunters use shotguns to shoot ducks. Shotguns fire shells instead of bullets. Shotgun shells contain small pellets called shot. A plastic or fiber container called a wad holds the pellets. Gunpowder inside a shell creates an explosive charge when hunters fire a shotgun. The charge pushes the wad out of the gun's barrel. The pellets then spread out in the air. Ducks fall if enough pellets hit them.

Duck hunters use various types of shotguns. Most duck hunters use double-barrel, pump, or semi-automatic shotguns.

shot—the pellets in a shotgun shell

Duck hunters use a variety of equipment.

Shotgun

Legend

1. Stock
2. Trigger
3. Safety
4. Discharge Chamber
5. Loading Chamber
6. Forestock
7. Barrel

Double-barrel shotguns have two barrels. Some double-barrel guns have barrels located side by side. Other double-barrels have one barrel on top of another. Hunters must place another shell in a double-barrel's chamber after firing.

Pump and semi-automatic shotguns work differently than double-barrels. Hunters can shoot a pump shotgun once. They then reload the gun by pumping the gun's forestock back and forth.

A semi-automatic shotgun is gas-operated. The explosive charge of a shell produces gas. The gas pushes the used shell out of the chamber. The gas also pushes a new shell into the chamber.

Duck hunters can buy shotguns with different gauges. A gun's gauge is the inside width of the barrel. Most shotgun gauges are measured in millimeters. Guns with low gauges are more powerful than guns with high gauges. Many duck hunters use 10- or 12-gauge shotguns. But some duck hunters use guns with gauges of 20 or more.

Shells

Shells have a hard outer coating made of plastic. The shell's bottom is covered with metal. Duck hunting shells are about 3 inches (7.6 centimeters) long.

EDGE FACT

Shot fired from a shotgun travels around 1,200 feet (365 meters) per second.

Duck hunters use non-toxic shells. These shells contain pellets made of steel, iron, or tin. In the past, duck hunters used shells with lead pellets. Lead pellets are poisonous. Many puddle ducks in heavily hunted areas died after they accidentally ate lead pellets. Today, it's illegal to hunt ducks with lead pellets in North America.

The shot inside of shells comes in different sizes. Large shot travels farther than small shot. But shells with large shot contain fewer pellets than shells with small shot.

Shells have different shot weights and strengths of powder. This combination is called load. Loads can be field, standard, or magnum. Field loads contain the most lightweight shot. They also have the least powder charge. Standard loads contain heavier shot and have more powder charge than field loads. Guns that have more powder charge produce more power.

Magnum loads contain the heaviest shot and have the greatest powder charge. These loads also spray pellets in a closer pattern than field or standard loads.

Decoys

Ducks often land to join other ducks. Hunters place decoys to attract ducks to their hunting areas. Duck decoys are made of wood, plastic, or rubber. Duck hunters usually place them in the water. Weights tied to the decoys prevent them from floating away. Hunters might place some decoys on land.

The type of decoy hunters use depends on the species they are hunting. Ducks are more likely to land near other members of the same species.

Boats

Duck hunters use different types of boats. Canoes are used on ponds, rivers, and marshes. Duck hunters might use jonboats. Jonboats have a square bottom. The square bottom helps hunters stand and shoot without tipping the boat over. Pirogues have pointed ends and a wide bottom. Pirogues are stable and easy to move in shallow areas. Large motorboats allow hunters to move quickly in large lakes and oceans.

Hunters try to hide their boats from ducks. They paint their boats to blend in with the surroundings. Hunters also slide their boats between tall plants.

EDGE FACT

In January 2007, a pair of hand-carved duck decoys, made around 1900, sold at an auction for $90,000.

Duck Hunting—Boats

Duck hunters build blinds to hide from ducks.

Blinds

Many duck hunters use natural features such as hills, rocks, grass, or weeds to hide from ducks. But they also might use their own hidden shelters. These shelters are called blinds. Some duck hunters purchase blinds from outdoor or sporting goods stores. Other duck hunters create blinds.

blind—a shelter that hunters use to hide from ducks

Duck hunters can create blinds in various ways. They might attach weeds or cornstalks to wire. In coastal areas, duck hunters use rocks or driftwood along the shore. Some duck hunters use strips of a coarse woven fabric called burlap. They attach the strips to metal netting. Burlap can protect hunters from wind and help keep them warm. Many duck hunters attach blinds to boats or rafts. Hunters hide in or behind blinds until ducks are close enough to shoot.

Other Equipment

Hunters also use duck calls. Hunters blow into these small plastic or wooden tubes to attract ducks. The air flowing through the calls makes sounds similar to the sounds of certain duck species. Duck hunters use calls designed for the species that they want to shoot. Duck hunters attach their calls to strings called lanyards. They wear the lanyards around their neck.

call—a device that makes a sound like a duck

Duck hunters wear chest waders to stay dry in the water.

Duck hunters should carry waterproof flashlights that float. Ducks are most active near sunrise and sunset. Hunters might be traveling to or leaving their hunting locations in the dark.

Some hunters carry a wing chart. This chart helps duck hunters identify the ducks they see.

Clothing

Duck hunters wear waterproof clothing. They wear waders to keep themselves dry. Waders are made of waterproof materials, such as rubber and nylon. They may be hip boots or chest waders.

Hip boots are waterproof pants attached to boots. They cover a hunter's legs and have straps that connect to a hunter's belt.

Chest waders cover a hunter's legs and upper body. They usually have straps that fit over the shoulders. Chest waders often have boots attached to them.

Many duck hunters wear nylon wind- and water-resistant jackets. Some duck hunters bring waterproof coats to protect them from rain. Duck hunters wear heavy coats, hats, and mittens or gloves in cold weather.

Most hunters wear camouflage clothing to hide from ducks. The colors of this clothing blend into the surroundings. Many hunters believe ducks are frightened by bright colors.

waders—long, waterproof boots

Essential Duck Hunting Equipment

Legend

1. Blind
2. Shotgun
3. Waders
4. Shells
5. Calls
6. Decoys

Chapter 3

SKILLS AND TECHNIQUES

Learn about jump shooting, how to attract ducks, and hunting dogs.

D uck hunters must learn to shoot properly. They practice shooting at saucer-shaped targets called clay pigeons.

Some hunters practice calling. Each duck species makes a different type of sound. Duck hunters practice making realistic calls.

Jump Shooting

Some hunters sneak up on ducks to shoot at them. This practice is called jump shooting. Duck hunters usually jump shoot while they hunt puddle ducks. These ducks rest on small bodies of water. It's easy for duck hunters to sneak up on ducks in these small areas.

EDGE FACT

Duck hunters compete at the National Duck Calling Contest each year in Stuttgart, Arkansas.

Some duck hunters shoot from blinds attached to boats.

Duck hunters who jump shoot might use binoculars to look for ducks. They carefully approach the ducks that they see. Hunters can hide behind trees, hills, tall bushes, or weeds. When they are close enough to shoot, they scare the birds into the air and shoot at them.

Attracting Ducks

Duck hunters use calls and decoys to attract ducks. Puddle duck hunters use calls more often than diving duck hunters do. Decoys sometimes attract diving ducks without calls.

The number of decoys duck hunters place in the water depends on the area's size. Duck hunters might place hundreds of decoys on large bodies of water. They use only a few on small bodies of water.

Duck hunters place decoys in front of them. Some of the decoys should be within shooting range. Most duck hunters place decoys less than 30 feet (9 meters) away from them.

Hunters sometimes leave one side of a decoy arrangement open. Ducks often land in open areas.

Duck hunters should consider wind conditions when they place decoys. Ducks normally fly into the wind as they land. They spread their wings before landing. The wind blowing against their wings slows down the ducks and helps them land. Hunters should face open areas of their decoy arrangements into the wind.

Duck hunters can place decoys in various arrangements. Duck hunters place decoys in a long "J" shape. The bottom of the "J" is closest to the hunters. Ducks will land in the curved, open bottom of the "J."

Duck Hunting—Arranging Decoys

Puddle duck hunters sometimes place decoys in two groups on either side of their location. Ducks then land between the two groups.

Puddle duck hunters also place decoys in a "C" shape. They face the opening of the "C" into the wind.

Diving duck hunters place long strings of decoys in the water. They put the decoys in a "V" shape. Diving ducks follow the path of decoys and land in the middle of the "V."

Shooting

Duck hunters must have good shooting technique to hit moving targets. They need to adjust their angle of shooting. They must consider the ducks' flight speed and make sure they are within shooting range.

Duck hunters use the swing-through technique. A hunter holds a gun with one hand behind the trigger and the other hand under the gun's forestock. The hand underneath the forestock raises the barrel while the other hand brings the end of the gun to the shoulder. Hunters swing the gun to aim ahead of the duck in its flight path.

The distance hunters leave between the duck and the barrel depends upon how fast the duck is moving, its angle, and the shooting range. The hunters then fire the gun in front of the bird. They keep moving the gun along the duck's line of flight after firing the gun.

Hunting Dogs

Duck hunters often use dogs to find and bring back ducks that are shot down. Dogs can find wounded ducks that otherwise might escape from hunters.

Hunting dogs must be properly trained. They must know how to sit, stay in one place, retrieve, and come when called. The dogs also need to sit quietly in a boat or blind.

EDGE FACT

Duck hunting dogs have to be trained to be unafraid of loud gunfire.

Duck Hunting Dog Breeds

Chesapeake Bays

Chesapeake bays originally came from areas surrounding Chesapeake Bay on the eastern coast of the United States. Chesapeake bays are various shades of tan or brown. The dogs may have a white spot on their chest, stomach, or paws. Chesapeake bays have a double coat. The inner layer is dense and long. The outer coat is short and smooth. These dogs work especially well in cold, icy conditions.

Labrador Retrievers

Labrador retrievers originally came from Canada. Many people call labradors "labs." Labradors are muscular dogs with short, smooth coats. Labs can be black, yellow, or brown. The brown coloring is called chocolate. Labradors have oily coats that shed water. They are good swimmers.

Golden Retrievers

Golden retrievers originally came from England and Scotland. They have thick coats. Golden retrievers' coats can be one of several shades. The color varies from light tan to gold-red. Golden retrievers are good swimmers.

Chapter 4

CONSERVATION

Learn about wildlife refuges, Ducks Unlimited, and bag limits.

R esponsible duck hunters practice good conservation habits. They take care of duck habitats. Some duck hunters join clubs and donate money to protect duck habitats.

Wetlands

Wetlands provide ducks with a place to nest. These areas of shallow water have many plants. Wetlands are located along rivers, near lakes, in coastal areas, and in large areas of grass called prairies. Ducks use the plants to hide their nests from predators such as foxes, raccoons, and coyotes. These animals eat duck eggs.

predator—an animal that hunts other animals for food

Duck hunters hunt in wetland areas.

People can help maintain areas where ducks nest.

One of the largest wetland areas in North America where ducks live is in central Canada and the northern United States. The area includes the Canadian provinces of Alberta, Saskatchewan, and Manitoba. The region extends south through the states of North Dakota, South Dakota, and Minnesota.

Duck Hunting—Protecting Wetlands

Protecting Wetlands

Many activities can harm or ruin wetlands. Water is drained from wetlands for crops. People also drain wetlands to build roads, homes, and office buildings.

Government agencies buy some wetlands to provide ducks with habitats. These agencies include the U.S. Fish and Wildlife Service and the Canadian Wildlife Service. Some wetlands owned by government agencies are refuges. Duck hunting is limited or illegal in these areas.

Government agencies also create programs to protect and restore wetlands. These programs clean polluted water areas and maintain structures where ducks nest.

In 1937, hunters formed Ducks Unlimited (DU). Since then, DU has preserved nearly 25 million acres (10 million hectares) of duck habitat in North America.

EDGE FACT —⊚∙ⓒ)

The United States lost more than 4 million acres (1.6 million hectares) of wetlands between 1975 and 1995.

refuge—a place that provides protection or shelter

Regulations

Government agencies in North America establish regulations to protect duck populations. The rules prevent too many ducks from being killed. The U.S. Fish and Wildlife Service establishes federal duck hunting regulations in the United States. This agency suggests regulations to state governments. But state governments establish most duck hunting regulations.

The Canadian Wildlife Service works with Canadian provinces to establish most regulations in Canada. But provinces also create additional hunting rules.

Government agencies also set limits on the number of ducks hunters can kill in one day. This number is called the daily bag limit.

North America also has duck hunting seasons. Hunters can only hunt between these dates in the fall. The season's length depends on the area's duck population. Southern states start their seasons later in the fall than northern states do. Ducks usually do not migrate through southern states until late fall.

bag limit—the number of ducks a hunter is allowed to kill in one day

Duck hunters can only hunt during hunting seasons.

Government agencies also set rules for youth duck hunting. Youth hunters must pass a gun safety class and hunt with an adult. Young hunters sometimes can hunt without a license. But hunters age 16 and older need a license. These hunters also need to purchase federal permits or stamps.

Chapter 5

SAFETY

Learn about gun safety, weather safety, and first aid.

S afety is important to duck hunters. Some hunters take gun safety classes. Hunters should also be aware of the weather conditions and their surroundings.

Gun Safety

Duck hunters should follow guidelines to make sure no one is accidentally shot. They always store guns unloaded. They never point a gun at another person or anything that they do not want to shoot. Duck hunters make sure they can see the target clearly before they shoot at it.

Duck hunters should put a gun's safety on when they are not using it. This device located near the trigger prevents a gun from firing.

safety—a lever on a gun that prevents the gun from firing

Duck hunters must be careful with their guns.

Other Safety Concerns

Other safety guidelines are important to duck hunters. Hunters in boats should wear life jackets. Duck hunters should hunt with another person. If one hunter is injured, the other can help.

Duck hunters should watch weather conditions. They should pay attention to weather reports and be aware if storms are in the area.

First Aid

Duck hunters should carry first aid kits in case they become injured. Items in first aid kits include scissors, gloves, medicine tape, and bandages. The kits also have gauze to cover wounds. Most kits have antibiotic ointment to protect wounds from germs.

Safe duck hunters are prepared for accidents. They know basic first aid skills and are careful with their guns. They know that being responsible can help everyone enjoy the sport.

Gun Safety

1. Treat all guns as if they were loaded.

2. Do not point a gun at anything you do not intend to shoot.

3. Identify the target before shooting. You should have a clear view of the target.

4. Keep the safety on until you are ready to shoot. Then keep your finger straight and off the trigger until you fire.

5. Keep the gun unloaded when you are not using it. Unload a gun immediately after you are finished using it.

6. Keep different bullets and shells separate from each other.

7. Do not shoot at hard surfaces. The bullets or shells could bounce off these surfaces and injure someone.

8. Always check to see what is beyond your target. A bullet or shell that misses the target may hit an object, person, or animal beyond the target.

9. If you fall, check to make sure the barrel is clear. A barrel that is blocked by an object might burst.

10. Do not lean a gun anywhere it may slip and fall.

North American Duck Species

Mallard

Description: Mallards are puddle ducks. They are the most commonly hunted North American ducks. Male mallards have a dark green head and a white band around their neck. They have a brown chest and a white underside. Female mallards are mostly brown with black spots. Mallards are 18 to 28 inches (46 to 71 centimeters) long. They weigh between 1.5 and 4 pounds (.7 and 1.8 kilograms).

Habitat: marshes, swamps, ponds, lakes, bays

Food: aquatic plants, seeds, insects, corn, wheat, soybeans

Wood Duck

Description: Wood ducks are puddle ducks. Male wood ducks have a bright green head. The head has a dark blue or black mask with white streaks. Male wood ducks also have a dull red chest, a green back, and a bright orange bill. Female wood ducks have a tan underside and a dark brown back. Their bill is gray with a black tip. Wood ducks are 15 to 21 inches (38 to 53 centimeters) long. They weigh between 1 and 2 pounds (.5 and .9 kilogram).

Habitat: swamps, ponds, rivers

Food: aquatic plants, acorns, corn, soybeans

Green-Winged Teal

Description: Green-winged teals are the smallest of all puddle ducks. They have dark green spots on their wings. Males have a dark green mask across their orange face. Their chest is tan with black spots. Females are tan with black spots. They have a dark brown streak across their eyes. Green-winged teals are 13 to 15 inches (33 to 38 centimeters) long and weigh between .5 and 1 pound (.2 and .5 kilogram).

Habitat: marshes, shallow lakes, ponds

Food: seeds, small aquatic animals, insects, corn, soybeans

Common Goldeneye

Description: Some people call common goldeneyes "whistlers." These diving ducks make a whistling sound as they fly. Common goldeneyes have a white throat and underside. Males have a black head, bill, back, and tail. They have a white spot behind their bill. Females have a brown head with no spot. Their sides are gray. Common goldeneyes are 16 to 20 inches (41 to 51 centimeters) long. They weigh between 1.5 and 3.5 pounds (.7 and 1.6 kilograms).

Habitat: shallow lakes and ponds, shallow bays along sea coasts

Food: small fish, aquatic plants

Make sure ducks are in range before shooting at them.

EDGE FACT ——⌒·☉

Don't set up right next to another hunting party. If you're not there first, find a different spot.

Duck hunters have to follow plenty of laws. Other "rules" are simply good sportsmanship. Below are some dos and don'ts that will help all duck hunters have a good season.

- Don't show up when the ducks do. Get there early. Other hunters will not be impressed when your noise drives away the ducks.
- Don't shoot at birds that are out of range. It's called sky-busting, and all it does is scare away other ducks.
- Don't shoot at another hunter's swing ducks. Swing ducks are closer to another hunter's area than yours but are making another "swing" around before landing. Let the other hunter take the shot.
- Do pick up your trash. Part of duck hunting is respect for the outdoors.
- Do treat other hunters as you would like to be treated.

GLOSSARY

camouflage (KAM-uh-flahzh)—coloring that makes hunters blend in with their surroundings

habitat (HAB-uh-tat)—the natural place and conditions in which animals live

migrate (MYE-grate)—to fly away at a certain time of year to live in a different area

refuge (REF-yooj)—a place that provides protection

regulations (reg-yuh-LAY-shuhns)—official rules

shell (SHEL)—the case that holds a gun's bullet or shot

shot (SHOT)—the pellets in a shotgun shell

species (SPEE-sheez)—a group of animals with similar features

waders (WAY-durz)—long waterproof boots used for fishing or duck hunting

READ MORE

Miller, Marie-Therese. *Hunting and Herding Dogs*. Dog Tales, True Stories about Amazing Dogs. New York: Chelsea Clubhouse, 2007.

Smith, Nick. *Waterfowl Hunting: Ducks and Geese of North America*. The Complete Hunter. Chanhassen, Minn.: Creative Publishing International, 2006.

Spencer, Jim. *A Young Hunter's Guide to Waterfowling and Conservation*. Memphis: Ducks Unlimited, 2004.

INTERNET SITES

FactHound offers a safe, fun way to find Internet sites related to this book. All of the sites on FactHound have been researched by our staff.

Here's how:

1. Visit *www.facthound.com*

2. Choose your grade level.

3. Type in this book ID **1429608188** for age-appropriate sites. You may also browse subjects by clicking on letters, or by clicking pictures and words.

4. Click on the **Fetch It** button.

FactHound will fetch the best sites for you!

INDEX